Creating Chances

Arts interventions in Pupil Referral Units and Learning Support Units

Richard Ings
Photographs by Adrian Fisk

CALOUSTE GULBENKIAN FOUNDATION

Published by
Calouste Gulbenkian Foundation
United Kingdom Branch
98 Portland Place
London W1B 1ET
Tel: 020 7908 7604
E-mail: info@gulbenkian.org.uk
Website: www.gulbenkian.org.uk

ISBN 1 903080 01 0

British Library Cataloguing-in-Publication Data
A catalogue record for this book is available from the
British Library

Designed by Andrew Shoolbred.
Cover designed by Onvisual, www.onvisual.com
Printed by Expression Printers Ltd, IP23 8HH

Distributed by Central Books Ltd, 99 Wallis Road,
London E9 5LN
Tel: 0845 458 9911, Fax: 0845 458 9912
E-mail: orders@centralbooks.com
Website: www.centralbooks.co.uk

Contents

Preface

In 2001 the Calouste Gulbenkian Foundation, in collaboration with Arts Council England, established the First Time Projects scheme. The purpose of the scheme was to offer small grants to teachers in Pupil Referral Units (PRUs) and Learning Support Units (LSUs) to enable them to initiate artists' residencies, based on the belief that practising artists often have much to offer pupils in these settings: they can introduce them sympathetically and authoritatively to new and creative skills, thus building up their confidence and self-belief; and they can gradually develop relationships with the pupils, helping them to improve their own ability to relate to others. Teachers, for their part, are able to witness and engage with these different processes and to begin to understand the particular value of creative activities for the pupils in their care. The overall purpose of the scheme, which ran in parallel with the Education Programme's well-established funding priorities in this field, was to stimulate the growth of such residencies across the whole sector.

The scheme ran for three years, receiving generous and welcome support from the Esmée Fairbairn Foundation in its second and third years. It attracted a total of 350 applications, dispensed £135,000 in grant aid and assisted nearly 50 projects throughout England. In the third year of the scheme there was a dramatic rise in the number of applications – a total of 209 compared to 81 in the previous year – which suggested that teachers were increasingly recognising the value of this work.

One way of encouraging the process further, we believed, would be to publish a short report on a selection of the projects funded under the scheme and to make it widely available to teachers in PRUs and LSUs, as well as to artists. What we had in mind was not a formal appraisal of each project, but a series of impressionistic accounts that would convey the day-to-day reality of arts residencies and speak to the uninitiated as well as to more experienced practitioners.

Arts activities in PRUs and LSUs can and do achieve as high a standard as arts activities in mainstream settings. However, their chief purpose is to provide opportunities for pupils' emotional and social development rather than to achieve excellence in an aesthetic sense, even if, in practice, these two outcomes can easily coexist. Evidence of a 'successful' arts project is primarily to be found in the *effect* that it has on the lives of the participants rather than in the activity itself. Discerning the effect, of course, is always difficult. Changes in a young person's attitude or behaviour can be subtle and elusive, barely visible except to those who know them well and can understand the significance of a word or gesture that may, on the face of it, seem insignificant. One of the strengths of Richard Ings's report is his ability to capture some of these moments of change, either first hand or from the testimonies of teachers, and to set them down. And such changes, the triggering of one sort of behaviour by another, the achievement of emotional growth through participation in an arts project, is at the heart of this work.

We hope that the teachers and artists who read this report and may be new to the kind of activities described here will be persuaded of their value, taking encouragement from the fact that all the teachers interviewed were novices once. We hope that the more experienced will find their horizons broadened and their understanding deepened, and that those with responsibility for policy are given an insight into the way in which arts activities delivered by professional artists have a very particular contribution to make to the lives of disaffected pupils.

Simon Richey
Assistant Director (Education)
Calouste Gulbenkian Foundation (UK Branch)

Introduction

How do pupils who have been at risk of exclusion from mainstream education, sometimes most of their school lives, react to the presence of artists – adults who bring often unorthodox methods of communication and expression into the classroom? How easy is it for teachers and other school staff to find common ground with artists and apply what they have learned from them to their own, more traditional relationships with young people? And how do artists themselves cope with the challenge of working with students who often have a limited attention span and who either define themselves by 'kicking off' – acting out their frustrations – or by withdrawing?

These were among the questions that occurred to me as I considered the brief I had been given by the Calouste Gulbenkian Foundation, and began to map out the visits I was to make to Pupil Referral Units (PRUs) and Learning Support Units (LSUs) over the following twelve months. As an observer, evaluator and writer on arts in schools projects for a number of years, I knew some of the basics about such work, and I also had some grasp of the particular issues involved in this sector from attending and reporting on the groundbreaking conference, The Arts Included, where the First Time Projects fund had been launched. Nevertheless, I had never visited such a project, nor had I been to see what a PRU or LSU was like, so this was virgin territory. I didn't know quite what to expect.

In the event, each visit I made further complicated my understanding of what these centres are like and what they are there for. LSUs, based on school campuses and with relatively easy access to mainstream activities and resources, are easier to pin down, though, in my small sample, even they varied from an ill-equipped set of rooms somewhere down a school corridor to a purpose-built 'learning centre' fully kitted out with computer hardware. PRUs are less uniform still, shape-shifting according to the particular policies of the local education authority, from virtual mini-schools with their own dedicated staff and tailored curricula to ragtag academies of the educationally dispossessed, every child stigmatised by academic, behavioural or medical abnormality. Each centre seems to have its particular angle on how far it will engage with the National Curriculum or on what kind of therapeutic approach it favours. Intake varies; outputs also vary. Yet, despite the enormous differences between these places where the 'disaffected' and disobedient are lodged, however temporarily, there are some common characteristics, at least in my limited observation.

One such feature is the evident closeness between staff and students. The pastoral element in the teacher's role, vestigial in some mainstream situations where the feverish accountancy of examinations and targets has taken hold, seems to blossom and flourish here. This may be partly because in some cases the children's parents themselves fail to provide sufficient care or take sufficient interest (itself, of course, a significant factor in the young person's thwarted development), so that *in loco parentis* takes on a more literal meaning than usual; I vividly remember one teacher commenting on how much some of her pupils dreaded Fridays and the last day of term. The closeness of the relationship is also, I am sure, a result of staff addressing the personal and social needs of the young person as much as or more than their academic needs. If there is a key at all to bringing such young people back into the educational or social fold, it surely lies in this care for 'the whole child'. Over and over again, staff – and artists working with them – identify a lack of self-esteem and confidence as the critical factor to overcome if these young people are going to rejoin their classmates, never mind realise their own potential, never mind spell properly and pass exams.

No doubt, with this parental closeness, PRUs and LSUs can replicate the fractured situation of a difficult home life. One centre rang apologetically to cancel my visit planned for the following day; all but one of its group of young people were being questioned by police about an 'incident' at the school. On another occasion, I was told that the regular teacher was off on 'stress-related leave', delaying the arts project. When I eventually spoke to her, it turned out that it was her pupils' treatment of the visiting artists that had so devastated her. This kind of crisis is, of course, a fact of life at such centres, unsurprising when antisocial behaviour is often the reason for students being here in the first place. For the most part, I only caught glimpses and whispers of such endemic problems on my visits: one boy, who had been happily showing me his computer graphic work that morning, turned silent after lunch when he had attacked another child; another described to me as courteous one minute – opening the door for staff and apologising for bumping into a teacher – and the next as breaking one pool cue after another in the games room or ripping a door off its hinges.

These situations, however, serve to illustrate another characteristic of these environments: the sheer unexpectedness and adventure of working here. Each day is different. Each day, no one is sure which students will turn up and, of those that do, who will really be up for it. More than one teacher confessed to me that they would never go back to 'mainstream' teaching now. The work in an LSU or a PRU is not safe, but neither is it hemmed in by the demands of the National Curriculum, the literacy and numeracy hours, the league tables and all the rest. At last, here there are small groups to work with. At last, there is time to experiment – a chance to try something a bit more creative.

Which brings us to *Creating Chances* and the arts projects that I describe in this book. From January to December 2003, I visited a dozen PRUs and LSUs, covering Years 1–11, across England – from St Helens on Merseyside to Guildford, from rural Yorkshire to the suburbs of South London. The projects, which lasted in some cases less than a term and in others a whole year or more, involved a variety of artists and artforms, from ceramicists to dancers, from making vinyl banners to devising drama. In some instances, around half a dozen young people were directly involved, in others a larger group took part – in one case, around a hundred pupils from across primary and secondary phases. What all these projects shared was that they were 'first time': this was something that the centres had never tried before, at least not with a live artist (or several) on site.

Although I prepared for my visits by reading about the projects and how they had been conceived, what they aimed to achieve and so on, and although I have in some cases discovered what progress has been made since, my engagement with each centre is largely confined to that one day's interviewing and observation.

There is a limit to what can be gleaned over a day, of course, but my brief has not been to attempt a full-scale evaluation of these projects. The aim is more modest: simply to provide an informed snapshot of this kind of work as it takes place, to capture it in mid-flow and bring into focus the teachers and support staff, the artists and the students as they engage with an activity whose outcome is yet to emerge. Although only full-scale tracking and longitudinal research will uncover just how lasting an impact such projects might have on the young people and the adult facilitators involved, I would argue that we can learn something of the value of arts interventions in PRUs and LSUs from shorter encounters.

Centre	Lead staff	Project description	Beneficiaries	Artist(s)
The Burlington Centre Newtown Birmingham PRU	Mandy Finney, Learning Support	A project aiming to produce posters containing poetry and photographic images on the theme of 'my community'	8 pupils aged 11–14	Levi Tafari, Poet David Petts, Photographer Karen McDonnell, Designer

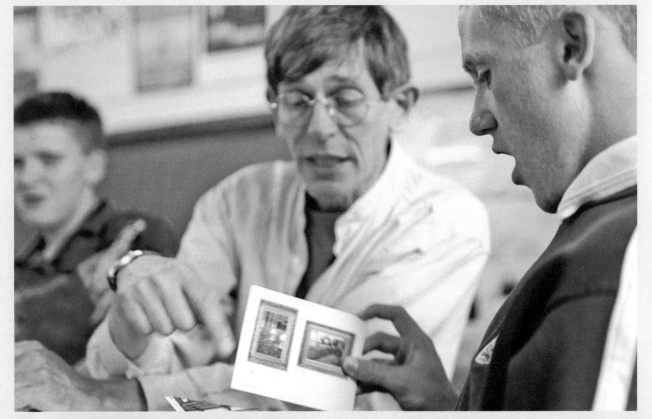

We learn for example, the way that the arts can provide a responsible and productive escape from the problems that have damaged so many of these young people; how engaging in creative work can restore a young person's sense of identity and purpose; the development of group and teamwork skills; the way in which such projects can connect young people with the adult community they will soon be entering; the possibility that projects like these can lead to the discovery of genuine artistic talent; the legacy that projects can leave among the teaching staff once the artist has left the building; the need to address emotional development as a prerequisite for teaching basic skills to these young people; the benefits of an integrated approach to curriculum and to target groups; the advantages of drawing on skills developed in other sectors, including youth and social work; and the separate but complementary roles of artist and teacher.

The observations that emerge from my informal encounters are, thus, both particular and general. Particular in the sense that every project has a unique chemistry, created by the participants and their relationships with each other, as well as by the art form (or forms) they have chosen to employ. General in the sense that the aims of all these projects duplicate and overlap each other, as do the outcomes for the participants in terms of personal and academic/professional development.

In each case, one or two main themes emerge, one or two aspects of this kind of work. Sometimes it is a chance remark from a participant, sometimes just a particular emphasis in the activity going on that day that crystallises such themes and provides a distinctive point of view. The following case studies, based on ten of my visits, are, therefore, not intended to be read as detailed and rounded assessments of each project but more as reports from the 'front line'. In a similar way, the images of the four other centres visited by photographer Adrian Fisk are not meant simply as a record of particular projects but to give the reader a visual impression of the concentration, creation and celebration that is characteristic of so many of them. There are epiphanies here, moments of transformation when chances are created and seized.

Together, I hope, these accounts will build cumulatively to provide the reader with a broader understanding of this work, an appreciation of the main issues and concerns that lie behind it, and an inkling of its many achievements, however fleeting or lasting they may prove to be.

■ ■ ■

I would like to thank all the members of staff, young people and artists who made my visits to PRUs and LSUs so stimulating and informative. Whilst the names of young people have been changed to protect their privacy, many of the adults who made me welcome are named in the text. To these, I would like to add special thanks to Juliette Buss of the Brighton Photo Biennial, who invited me to sit in on an artists' evaluation meeting with photographers Polly Arnett and Tom Wichelow, following a project she had managed involving the Brighton and Hove Learning Support Service; and to Yvette Unsworth who allowed me to participate in a staff training day, making masks with artist Zara Conway, at the Primary Learning Achievement Centre in West Kensington, midway through yet another successful project. These visits added considerably to my own knowledge of what kind of impact this work can have in terms of artists' and teaching staff's personal and professional development.

Richard Ings

1 Enough help, but not too much

Centre	Lead staff	Project description	Beneficiaries	Artist(s)
Integrated Support Service Centre Langdon Hills Basildon Essex PRU	Sharon Wilson, Assistant Manager Tim Moynihan, Senior Teacher Neil Finbow, ICT Maggie Torrie, Drama Sue Reeves, English Anne Ash, Art Sue Charlton, Primary and Music	Cultural Fusion, a series of multi-disciplinary arts workshops run over half a term on the theme of Africa and the Caribbean	80–100 pupils aged 5–16	Charlie Wilson, Storyteller Sol Ogundipe, The Afro Centre Mick Hutton, Musician (steel pan) Scott Irving, Graffiti artist Thabani Nyoni, Wise Moves Dance Malo Sonka, Drummer Heritage Ceramics

The Integrated Support Service Centre in Langdon Hills, Basildon is based in an old primary school. A long corridor runs right through the middle of the main block, before turning off towards the art department. There are display boards and pictures all along its walls. One board contains writing by pupils about the Cultural Fusion project.

> It was fun on paper but even more fun outside with a spray can. When I went wrong, which I did about a hundred times, Scott said don't worry about it and in the end it looked great. I was happy with it.
>
> Robert

> I enjoyed it because it was something new from what I normally do. Thabani showed us a street-dance routine and we done it with him a couple of times to the song *It's Getting Hot in Here* by Nelly. I hope I get the chance to do this another time.
>
> Louise

> Today we did some cooking with Stanley – yams, plantain and mangoes – never tasted them before. Asked my mum if I could cook some sweet potatoes at home.
>
> Simon

The teacher in charge of this PRU, Sharon Wilson, explains that Black or Asian people are rarely seen in this part of Essex; it is a very white area. According to one of the two girls I interview after lunch, there were some black students here at one time, but not now.

With a working group of around half a dozen teachers, including one (Tim Moynihan) who had run a successful Hindu wedding project a year earlier, Sharon began on a long and well-planned path to realising a major project about Africa and the Caribbean. The aim was not simply to give the whole Centre a good taste of a different culture and continent – ambitious enough, given the context – but to challenge the kind of knee-jerk racism common to largely mono-cultural communities. By now, all the pupils have 'touched' the project at least two or three times and have met some of the artists invited in to run workshops – a first for most of them and, in terms of working with guest artists, a first for the Centre.

Alongside artists' sessions on Caribbean cooking, African drumming, graffiti art, street and African dance, the black oral tradition and steel pan, students have also been learning about many other aspects of African life and culture as part of their normal lessons. Every department has participated, even Maths, where the teacher researched African counting games. Environmental issues affecting Africans – particularly water – have been brought into class discussion. Tim was already teaching about slavery in his class, aware that for many of the students Africa was just a vaguely conceived jungle. The unexpected discovery of a new organisation, called the Afro Centre, virtually on their own doorstep, was perfect timing; it was able to provide a range of useful resources. By bringing in artefacts and running creative workshops, staff at the Afro Centre broadened pupils' understanding of Africa, revealing the vastness of the continent and its endless variety, its cities as well as its jungles.

To make a complex project like this work as effectively as possible, planning is essential, and not just in researching, engaging and timetabling suitable artists. The nature of the 'clientele' is such that a badly planned project could end up damaging children and artists alike. If you are going to do this sort of project, Sharon believes, you need to take your time.

> Because we didn't rush the planning and because we concentrated the activities into this half of term, it has worked. They haven't got fed up.

■ ■ ■

The Support Centre, whose aim is to reintegrate pupils back into mainstream school, has a wide intake within a 20-mile radius: around 80 young people in all, though, as some are not full-time, there are between 40 and 50 on-site at any one time. Some of these pupils are now entitled to 25 hours contact time per week. There are four main groups of young people from both primary and secondary phases; most do not attend mainstream school. There are pregnant young girls and young mothers with babies. There are excluded

pupils; those at Key Stage 4, although based at another centre, attend some lessons here as well. There are children who are school-phobic and who have psychological problems; these form the biggest group here. To the uninitiated, this group might seem to be the easiest to deal with, but such withdrawn young people are often the most intractable; the girls in particular are prone to depression. Finally, there is a short-term population of pupils with medical problems, from juvenile arthritis to severe asthma, that prevent them from fully participating in mainstream schooling; in the past the Centre has had wheelchair-users.

Sitting in Sharon's office, listening to her reel off this long list of casualties, the Centre sounds less an educational establishment than a convenient place to dump anyone who doesn't easily fit into the mainstream system. Meeting some of the staff, talking to the pupils and simply strolling down that long corridor to look at the outstanding African-inspired artwork that the Centre has produced is enough to make me quickly revise that initial impression. There is a palpably happy atmosphere here, an unmistakable sense of busy-ness and purpose in the way that people move around the building.

The sense I get of an unusually positive ethos may derive not simply from the Centre's strong focus on education, but also from the somewhat controversial policy the Centre has towards integrating its disparate 'clients', not least through projects like Cultural Fusion.

> Generally, we integrate. Of course, there is a school of thought that we shouldn't even have these different ages and groups on the same site. We do tend to keep primary and Key Stage 3 pupils separate for lessons, but then we mix them together for projects like this, whether they are excluded or here for another reason. Rather than putting all the exclusions in one group and expecting the poor artist to deal with that lively situation, we put them in with the other pupils. That way, they are more likely to behave themselves.

An anecdote about a recent HMI visit does suggest that the categories they are assigned to by authority mean relatively little to the young people themselves.

> An inspector was here last term and he was concerned about our practice of putting delicate pupils with medical problems alongside children who have been excluded. Then he asked one of them – who had ME – how he felt about sitting next to an excluded pupil. 'I never have,' came the reply, although he was indeed sat right next to one.

If the sense of a community is strong here, it is also partly because the Centre is run as a tight ship. As in other centres, there is a policy of zero tolerance towards antisocial behaviour and bad language. Sessions such as the graffiti workshop are limited to more responsible students and sufficient staff are on hand to maintain control. The way in which this whole arts project was executed also suggests firm organisation and a steady weighing of the risks and benefits of such interventions.

In the event, it has been very successful, more so than Sharon or Tim expected. Pupils are now used to these unusual visitors and look forward to the next taste of African culture – not that this is always obvious to artists during the session. For example, Charlie Wilson, a well-known professional storyteller with personal links to the Centre (he is married to Sharon), found the response to his lively performance of African tales surprisingly muted.

> He didn't get the vibes back that he would normally get with children of that age, but they did really enjoy it. They just don't give out what children normally do. The excluded pupils can be way over the top, but many of the others simply sit there, not reacting, not joining in. They can't let themselves go, but, afterwards, they will say it was great – and mean it. The pregnant girls and young mothers, for instance, came out and said proudly that they had had a private viewing and that they were going to go back in for more.

Indications that some contact has been made, that there has been some kind of breakthrough are often virtually invisible to anyone not experienced in working with such children. Jack, for example, going up to Scott Irving, the graffiti artist, to thank him, unprompted, for the workshop which he had enjoyed was a highly significant moment. Jack has extreme anger management problems; despite this, he showed great concentration during the workshop.

Lisa and Jo from Year 11 also participated in creating the graffiti piece and were full of praise for Scott's approach.

> After we designed it, he drew it out in rough. We then filled it all in and did everything else. We did the whole piece in a single day. Scott was nice – he gave us enough help, but not too much.

The tact and skill implied here – allowing the young people to take creative responsibility – was shown by other artists, who would, in the girls' words, 'talk *to* you, not *at* you'.

> We liked the hands-on stuff, not just reading about it. Having artists in made it easier. They told us what we were doing wrong but it was different from teachers telling us what to do and what not to do. It was a laugh – instead of going to lessons, we've had something fun to do half-way through the week. It helps break things up.

■ ■ ■

Sharon and the other staff have been collecting a whole archive of material produced by the students both in class and in workshops. Some of this material will be included, along with selections from lengthy video footage and 'hundreds' of photographs taken of the project, in a pack that the Centre is publishing for other PRUs in the region. The purpose of the publication is not simply to record and celebrate the project but, more importantly, to encourage other centres to try the same approach: careful long-term planning and focused activity supported by all the staff.

This does not mean, of course, that the Centre has a magic formula. There is always an element of risk in bringing artists in. In this case, by taking their time and doing the necessary research, staff managed to secure the right people for the job. One such person is Mick Hutton, who is in today, in the next-to-last session of the project, to show students the possibilities of steel pan.

As it happens, back in the 1960s Mick was himself 'chucked out of school' at the age of 15. He then blew his chance of musical tuition at Colchester Institute by refusing his eminent tutor's request to get a haircut. His real education came the hard but effective way, through developing his musical skills in session work and earning his keep by working on London Underground, labouring, delivering coal. These days he plays regularly with Humphrey Lyttleton and has worked with everyone from Nigel Kennedy to Jack Bruce, with over 50 CDs to his credit. He now wants to focus more on this kind of education work, believing that his own experience in teaching himself the skills he has needed – from playing trombone and double bass to repairing car engines – can somehow be applied in the classroom.

Working with the students here is not that different from working with any young people, Mick reckons, though he could easily tell which of the group this morning had been excluded.

They give up so easily. I just can't do this, they say, and yet there they are, doing it. I can see real potential in these young people and yet I know it may never be realised. But that's our education system in a nutshell, isn't it?

Nevertheless, Mick's work and that of the other artists in the Cultural Fusion project, will, Sharon believes, strengthen the Centre's continuing efforts to raise the odds and bring that long untapped potential into play.

2 The importance of sketchbooks

Centre	Lead staff	Project description	Beneficiaries	Artist(s)
Primary Assessment Centre for Education (PACE) St Helens Merseyside PRU	Margaret Simpson, Teacher in charge	A project based around a number of textile techniques, including felt making and collage, with inset sessions	16 pupils aged 7–11	Amy Robinson, Textile artist

Rather than having to write down what they are feeling, they can simply draw it.

Every member of staff and every child at the Primary Assessment Centre for Education in St Helens now carries a sketchbook around. If textile artist Amy Robinson had her way, it would be standard practice to issue sketchbooks to all students, in or out of mainstream schooling.

> As an artist, I use sketchbooks all the time – they are so important. So many of our schools in St Helens don't have them, partly because of cost and partly because the thought simply doesn't occur to them. They don't understand the value of a sketchbook or how it can be used. It can show the progression of an idea and it can act as a visual diary. These children demonstrate brilliantly how therapeutic using it can be.

The sketchbooks in question are not large but could be fitted easily into a raincoat pocket or satchel. They are much in evidence in the classrooms of this centre, and are proffered, by teachers and by pupils, as proof of a continuing engagement with visual exploration. The appearance of the finished artwork on display – including painted masks and dolls – and of the large textile hanging, which is in progress as I arrive, can all be traced back to sketches and doodles in the children's sketchbooks, many of them crammed with glued-in materials including scraps of cloth and dried flowers.

As Amy implies, the contents are not simply experiments or dry runs at producing artwork but they can also illustrate personal journeys and experiences. Just as Amy had begun her residency by sharing her own sketchbooks with students and talking about the importance of relationships in her own art, Leo came to her one morning with a page of his book covered in smiling faces. He had clearly had an especially happy weekend with his family and wanted to depict – and share – that feeling. 'I knew you'd like that,' he said, satisfied with Amy's response.

■ ■ ■

The Centre – known as PACE for short – is a primary PRU. All its pupils have been assessed by staff going out to visit them at their mainstream schools; that link is maintained by returning pupils to their schools for a set two days each week. Initially, children will spend two full weeks here, to get them used to the system, but there is no desire to keep them full time after that, as the purpose is to reintegrate them into their mainstream schools. According to Margaret Simpson, the teacher in charge of PACE, many children find it 'safer' here than back in their own schools so reintegration can be a challenge.

Part of that sense of safety may lie in the system set up by PACE to create boundaries and structures for behaviour. The Centre is an enthusiastic subscriber to the notion of rewards and demerits, endorsed, they point out, by many educational psychologists. A complex awards system has been devised, in which points are given not just for adherence to ordinary school rules but for meeting specific individual targets, such as a wandering child managing to stay at their desk to work for a specific period. Children can earn anything from a Kit-Kat to (with enough points) a trip out ten-pin bowling. 'Things I might let pass,' says Amy, who has considerable experience of working in schools, 'are treated differently here – it's quite interesting to know where the boundaries are set.'

I witness an example of this ethos of social responsibility when I join a class for its regular late afternoon session, known as Meeting. Basically a circle group, it gives children and staff the chance to mull over and discuss the good and less positive aspects of their day. An initial prayer sets the tone for such contemplation.

■ ■ ■

The rules for art are less clear cut than those for acceptable social behaviour. It is not, Amy maintains, a question of 'this is wrong, that is right'. Art is more blurred than that and this is a big advantage in this kind of developmental work.

> A lot of these children have no confidence. When they've done a drawing, they often say it's horrible. I point out to them the good things in their picture, trying to show them that in no way is it 'rubbish'. I tell them that we are not trying to produce photographs with these drawings but simply trying to express ourselves.

Constant positive affirmation of the quality of their work is vital, according to Amy, if they are to make progress, or produce anything at all. Of course, this does not mean that art is simply a free-for-all, where anything goes. There is discipline here, too, as the children discovered in their first task with Amy. Creating the large mural now on display in the hall was the artist's initial strategy for engaging their interest.

If we started off with anything too small, it might have been restrictive. I thought that going straight into something as big as this, so that everyone could see how good it was, would boost their confidence and get our relationship off to a good start. We began with doing a lot of drawing around our theme – other cultures – and then the children did the whole thing from scratch: priming the MDF board, sizing it up by eye and using chalk – no other tool – and then painting it. At first, they were splashing paint about everywhere but with my help they became a bit more controlled and now they can mix and use paint really well.

The fear – even the expectation – of failure is one of the constant themes to emerge from meeting young people in settings like this. What Amy has tried to do, with visible success, is persuade pupils to take risks, in the belief that art provides a safe space where 'mistakes' can enhance learning rather than bring it, unpleasurably, to a halt.

■ ■ ■

Breaking off from work on a growing tapestry, Amy and the half dozen or so pupils in the class, together with teacher and classroom assistant, engage in what has become a regular exercise to generate new imagery. My formality already compromised by wearing a large checked shirt over my suit (kindly offered to protect me from splashes of paint), I now, along with the whole group, shut my eyes and draw the first thing that comes into my head as Amy intones 'Ding dong merrily on high…', first with my normal drawing hand and then with my left. Amy gently chides one or two pupils for 'drawing too small again' – my attempts at angels and church spire look positively microscopic – and we try larger gestures with the next line of the Christmas carol.

While the children develop what they have done on rough paper into more detailed images in their sketchbooks, I ask Amy the purpose of this drawing in the dark.

> We did it a lot at the beginning of the project because it's fun and because no one can be

expected to create a flawless drawing with their eyes shut. In fact, by using a continuous line, you might actually produce something better – by concentrating on the mental image you are not distracted by the object itself.

Such exercises aim to dispel a fear around creativity, shared by teachers, too.

> Teachers, especially in primary schools if they are not specialists, are usually scared of doing anything 'arty'. But we are all arty to some degree, whether it's in our appreciation of colour or pattern or whatever. They think they can't draw, assuming that a drawing has got to be really difficult and complex. In fact, as I tell them in Inset sessions, when I am handing out sketchbooks, it can often be very simple and still look fantastic.

■ ■ ■

One of the highlights of the residency for Amy was a teacher telling her that they loved the sketchbooks so much that they were going to keep on using them. Talking to the teachers of the two groups that Amy had been working with over the term, it became clear to me that this was an expression of a wider legacy that the project and this artist would be leaving at PACE.

> This project finishes in December, but it won't really, because the ideas that Amy has given the staff and the pupils are going to go on forever. We have been totally inspired.

It is part of Amy's practice to try to leave a school with skills that can be carried on – staff here have all learnt felt-making, for example – and she believes that a lot of good in-service training happens 'when you're working alongside the children'. Staff have already surprised the artist by working on a project on their own initiative, applying the lessons they had learned to designing and making dolls on a Nativity theme.

■ ■ ■

By spreading her time out over the term, rather than doing an intensive, hit-and-run residency, Amy has become a familiar figure in the Centre and has won the trust of the children. She asked permission right at the start to join the children for breakfast at 8.45 a.m., so that they could get to know her. Knowing that many of the children here have short attention spans, she learned to be more flexible with activities than in her mainstream sessions, making changes when children became fed up. It is significant that, asked to choose another highlight from the project, Amy recalls a visit a couple of weeks earlier when the older of the two groups, aged 10–11, stayed 'on task' for the whole day. Although fleeting and leaving no visible trace, this achievement seems to be as much a measure of the success of the project as the bulging sketchbooks held out to me by eager hands and the final work that will go on display at the end of term.

3 The green dot

Centre	Lead staff	Project description	Beneficiaries	Artist(s)
Didcot Girls' School Didcot Oxfordshire LSU	Sarah Pignéguy, Support Centre Coordinator	A project to make a film about living in Didcot	9 pupils aged 13–15	Elise Ahmed, RAP Community Action Ltd

The initial activity for this project was to make a map of the town using a huge sheet of graph paper and cutting out pictures from magazines. Everybody gets sticky dots. The red dots go on something they don't like, yellow dots on what they do like, and green dots on a place they'd like to change. We talk about their choices and the reasons for them. The playing fields, for example, may be dangerous because of the 'druggies', so on goes the red dot. Or they may want to put a green dot on the school. Working like this on the area they all live in has helped to bring them together as a team.

The team that film-maker Elise Ahmed, from RAP Community Action Ltd, is talking about is composed of four girls from the Pupil Support Centre at Didcot Girls' School and five selected from other classes at the school, all aged 13–15. The project she is discussing is Our Didcot; with Elise's expert guidance, the pupils are making their own video about what it is like living in this small Oxfordshire town. Most of the video has been shot on location.

The timing is serendipitous, as dramatic change is very much in the air in Didcot. The town, on first acquaintance, seems some way short of any architectural distinction or urban liveliness. But, as the pupils discovered when they were granted an interview with the Mayor and the Town Centre Manager, there are exciting plans for the place. I do wonder if Elise is overstating it, but, according to her, the overall plan is to 'knock the whole town down and rebuild it'. Clearly, someone somewhere has access to very large green dots.

■ ■ ■

'My uncle worked there,' one of the girls tells me as we take a brief tour of a silent and largely deserted industrial estate. She is pointing at an empty warehouse. There are half a dozen of us here, plus a video camera, all under the wing of Sarah Pignéguy, Coordinator of the Support Centre. We take some establishing shots in the neighbourhood before returning to base, where Sarah tells me about the Centre's brief history.

While some schools designate whole annexes – 'with toilets' – for their learning or pupil support units, there wasn't even a room available the day that Sarah first arrived, fresh from working at a PRU. The room where we are now sitting, along with a teaching assistant and a few girls, was once the domain of a maths teacher.

The Centre has been running for nearly two years. Initially, it supported half a dozen Year 10 girls who had been regularly truanting. One moved on to one day a week in college and a work placement at a local hairdresser's that has now turned into a full-time job. Three managed to sit their exams successfully. One, who came from a family where no one had gone to school, was lost completely: 'She'd come in and do a little work and then come in again three weeks later. As she wasn't prepared to access any of the activities or opportunities we offered her, there was really nothing else we could do for her.'

The current pupils are just as varied. Catherine, for example, comes to the Centre for just one lesson, to get the week off to a good start; she then attends normal lessons. Another girl, by contrast, would come in just for breakfast; dressed in jeans, she felt safe – wearing uniform is compulsory in the rest of the school. That couldn't last and she has now stopped coming in altogether, yet the Centre's story is largely one of success: almost all the pupils here do some mainstream lessons, often accompanied by a Learning Support Assistant. There is a range of formal activities and creative projects geared to specific pupils' needs, according to Sarah, 'all aimed at providing therapy in the school context'. These include, for example, literacy projects based on novels or films and fabric painting to create cushion covers. Living skills – dealing with issues such as anger management – are as much a focus as more academic or creative skills.

I ask Sarah how teaching in this sort of centre differs from working at a PRU.

> Our work with pupils is exactly the same – we are dealing with the same sort of needy young people – but at a PRU there are not the constraints we have at school with everyone on different timetables, having to wear uniforms and all the rest of it. We can't be as flexible here. However, it is better for pupils to stay in touch with a mainstream school. At the PRU it was difficult to access GCSEs – here at least they are more in touch with a wider range of lessons. And it's good for them to stay with their peer group.

Elise has been working with young people like these for far less time than Sarah – three years – but she also knows that there are no magic answers: 'A lot of it is just down to liking young people, valuing them, wanting to hear what they have got to say, and being confident in what *I* do.'

She knows the value of video in involving young people: 'they always want to have a go, even if some are a bit shy to start with.' Editing has been, if anything, more empowering than shooting.

> It is such a powerful process. It would have been unfair to do it on my own. They were able to decide how they wanted the film to look, what music to put on it, what order they wanted the sequences in. It is a really time-consuming process, so I had to do some of it myself – but I made sure that it reflected what they wanted.

Talking to the girls confirms that this has been a significant learning experience. They have found out how to use this equipment. One girl told me that she had not used any kind of camera before.

> It was confusing at first – what to press, what not to press. Now I've got my own camera at home and I'm messing round with Mum and Dad, recording family videos.

Two others vividly remember using the stop action of the camera to create a 'comic strip' effect. Sarah is also impressed at what other skills have been developed in the process of making the video – gaining confidence by going out and about with the equipment, being responsible, getting local people to talk to them on camera, and learning to work together as a team. As one girl said to me: 'We all listen to each other now.'

■ ■ ■

The main action on the project – and other activities including dance and visual art – take place off site, at a local youth centre. I am walked over there for lunch by two of the pupils. This centre is rather better equipped; pupils are making pizzas in the kitchen area and the walls are covered in artwork and the usual colourful cautionary posters. Sarah joins us just as I am proudly presented with a fresh pizza with all the toppings.

> The youth centre is a great venue for us. The boundaries in youth work and school are so different. If you want to do things that are loud and expressive, it wouldn't be fair to do

them in schools where the teachers would be tempted to tell them off or discipline them. It would confuse everyone's boundaries. They know this place is different, so they relax a lot more and open up.

School feels a lot more than a ten-minute walk away. And the girls seem a little more confident here. Their body language is different. While it will not be long before some of them will be leaving school, in many ways they still need mothering.

While Elise took them out, I stayed behind and did the rations for when they came back – sandwiches and soup. We set up a rota for the groups and it became an integral part of the project – one we hadn't expected. To

have them all cooking and sitting round the table eating together is something they don't do at home. Some of them don't know even the simplest things – like washing your hands before you eat.

Yet, these young women have also been out with their camera and microphone, canvassing the general public and winning council support and funding for developing their project. They have got much more involved in the wider, adult community and more interested in the future of their own town.

There isn't anything for them to contribute here normally, so it's given them a real sense of pride to be able to show audiences *their* Didcot.

Centre	Lead staff	Project description	Beneficiaries	Artist(s)
Pupil Referral Service North Secondary Brookside Mobile Unit Lancaster PRU	Frances Holland, Teacher	A 6-week project, Soundcard, based on songwriting, percussion and the production of a recording	10 pupils aged 11–14	More Music, Morecambe

4 Out of fire and earth

Centre	Lead staff	Project description	Beneficiaries	Artist(s)
The Pewley Centre Guildford Pupil Referral Unit Surrey PRU	Pippa Morris, Head of Centre	Creating a large tile mural for the entrance of the PRU through 12 one-day workshop sessions	16 pupils aged 11–14	Liliana Montoya, Ceramicist

Liliana Montoya's house is halfway down a narrow cul-de-sac of 1930s red-brick terraced cottages. Filing down a side alley, we emerge in a pleasant, sunny garden where a table and benches have been erected on the lawn, with soft drinks and cakes laid out for us. Liliana comes forward to greet us warmly; her husband Carlos emerges briefly from the dark interior of the studio to add his own shy welcome. We make a large group – Pippa Morris, who is Head of the Pewley Centre, half the pupils involved in the project and three members of staff. As we refresh ourselves, some of us wander around the garden and examine the totem-like and vividly coloured ceramic sculptures that Liliana and her husband have created here. Some of these, she tells us, have been exhibited internationally; one, which was entered for a competition in Bilbao, bears a poem in Spanish by Pablo Neruda. Circling round the pot to translate it for me, Liliana says that it is a poem about how hands can transform the earth through fire.

It is quiet here, apart from an occasional train rumbling out of Guildford station, which lies somewhere beyond the end of the garden.

■ ■ ■

This is by no means the first time that pupils from Guildford PRU have met ceramicist Liliana. Today is roughly the mid-point of the project they have been working on and the moment that the artist has chosen to introduce them to her own studio and the working life she shares with Carlos.

The project is about decorative tiles. A mural of welcome is planned for the entrance to the Centre, which is based in an old-style primary school building. The mural will be composed of traditional square tiles, each individually made, painted and glazed by pupils aged 11–14. The first phase of the project has been to familiarise the students – over a dozen of them – with the history and function of tiles. This has necessitated an early trip or two away from the Centre. One was to Guildford Museum, where staff allowed pupils to handle seventeenth-century Delft tiles, a gesture of trust that had clearly impressed the young people.

> It was good, being able to hold the tiles. They were blue and white, made ages ago. They even let us hold one there wasn't a matching copy of.

The museum also offered to put the proposed mural on display before it was installed at the Centre in the autumn. Pupils then went to see a tile collection held at Compton Art Gallery.

Another visit was to a little-known museum in Godalming, built at the turn of the last century for art nouveau artist G.F. Watts by his wife. It seems that she was very interested in what we would now call community arts and she had involved the whole village in a project to tile and decorate the local church.

One of the young people recalls a fourth visit – to some public toilets in Guildford. This was, in fact, to see some of Liliana's own tiles *in situ*. Since then, the pupils have been working with Liliana and staff to sketch out ideas for tile designs.

> Up to now we have been trying to give them the creative elements they need, building up geometrical, figurative elements. I want them to be familiar with these before we come to do the big mural. It is important for them to understand how long the process is. That is why I arranged this visit now rather than at the beginning, as it is about the next stage: painting and glazing tiles and getting them fired in the kiln. After today, I hope that they realise that this is not an immediate thing but a process that takes time.

■ ■ ■

'Would you like to come inside and look at my studio?' Liliana asks us. She promises a demonstration by Carlos of how to paint a tile. She apologises half-heartedly for the untidiness of this 'Aladdin's cave', but it is, as she says, a workshop after all. 'Do you get lots of spiders in here?' asks one of the pupils. Pots, tiles and ceramic sculptures, tools and sketches fill the benches and walls. Fascinated, we troop into the studio, which is divided into two rooms. In the back is the kiln, which Liliana later explains can heat up to 1300 degrees and which takes a whole day to cool down before the fired pots or tiles can be removed. She begins by describing the glazing process and the way colours change during firing. The colour of the paint that Carlos is now applying to create a sun picture on a blank tile, for example, bears little resemblance to the colour it will be once it has been in the kiln.

> We're painting today with something called cobalt oxide – do you know what that is? It's a metal which turns blue when it is heated up. That's why I like making ceramics: there is always that element of magic. Some colours, like yellow, actually disappear if they get too hot so you have to be careful in setting the tempera-

ture. One of the things about being a ceramic painter is that you have – almost – to guess at the eventual colour it will turn out to be because you can never really see it while you are doing it. You have to use your imagination a lot.

Liliana points at a detailed copy of what looks like one of those Delft tiles, covered in a range of blue tones. She says that it probably took Carlos a couple of days to work out how to achieve all those different shades. 'It would take me about a year', murmurs one of the students, impressed. All through our tour of the studio, students have been asking questions, about the detail of the process, their participation in it, and also about Liliana's life as an artist.

Having demonstrated just how many stages have to be gone through before a tile is ready – 'Always keep in mind,' she says, 'that this is a long process, quite different from drawing something on a piece of paper' – Liliana brings us all out into the garden, where pots of thin greyish-looking paint and brushes have replaced the plates and glasses on the table. It is now the students' turn to have a go at creating their own sun designs on blank tiles. Liliana has already reassured one girl that if it goes wrong, she can simply turn the tile over and start again.

Malcolm takes the bold step of volunteering to draw first, not easy under the gaze of the rest of us, but soon he and his classmates have relaxed into activity.

■ ■ ■

On the first day of the project, Liliana gave pupils a 'kit', which included a sketchbook, a diary, a little case with coloured pencils and other useful materials; this was something for them to keep. Tangible items are, she believes, important for children like these, who suffer from 'a complete lack' of self-confidence.

> They always want to know what they will 'get out of it'. It's not enough to say that there will be a wonderful mural or that the Mayor will be along to open it. That's a bit abstract at this stage. They need to see physical things. If you are working with kids from a PRU, you need to gain their trust and confidence. It might sound like you're trying to buy that trust but all you're

doing by giving them a treat is giving them the sense that they are worth something. That's what our jaunts out to galleries and giving them tea and cake here are all about – making them feel better about themselves.

She contrasts her work here with teaching at the Bow Arts Trust in London's East End, where she can take a more directive role, asking students to do things in the confidence that they will do them.

Today you saw model behaviour, but I don't know what you will see this afternoon [when the group will be working back at the PRU on designs]. It changes from one session to another. It's incredible. They get frustrated very easily. As soon as that happens, it spirals out of control – the other day, one student had had enough and threw his chair across the room. A lot of them bicker and talk about each other in a very open and graphic way, which can be unpleasant to hear; they just don't have those boundaries most of us have. Today, though, I felt that they really trusted me. It was the first time they've said thank you to me. Yes, the work is hard and at the end of the day my mind wants to blow up with concentrating so hard and giving them so much encouragement, but I love the results. Every time I finish a session with them, I feel euphoric.

■ ■ ■

Liliana has been wanting to do a project like this for the past three years. It has been a long haul, getting people interested. Confusion over an Arts Lottery grant (first promised and then, when it turned out that the regional coffers were empty, summarily withdrawn) meant that an earlier version of the project, which would have involved an LSU in a school in Ash and resulted in a council-backed public sculpture, had to be scrapped. However, when she then heard about the First Time Projects fund, Liliana was able to take her desired collaboration with the Guildford PRU forward. The success of this project will, she believes, provide the basis for more sustained developments with a greater number of young people at risk of exclusion.

Liliana is unusual in taking on the role of project manager; all the other projects I have visited have been coordinated and run by teaching or specialist PRU staff. She suspects that such staff rather welcome someone else taking charge for a change. She has considerable experience as a teacher and workshop leader, and has often worked with young people, both at LSUs and in mainstream schools. She is a fervent believer in the educational value of young people working with artists and of participating directly in the creative process. She is, therefore, prepared to do a lot of the hard work that makes projects such as these possible: finding collaborators, persuading funders, coming up with practical arrangements that will make the best use of everyone's time and skills.

Though she leads the project right through to writing up the evaluation, Liliana maintains a clear line between her role and that of the teachers and classroom assistants in the project. She likes coming in, not as a conventional teacher, but to spark something off that teachers can then develop with the students. She is also wary of knowing too much of the children's personal histories.

I don't want to be prejudiced by that kind of knowledge. My role is to come in and offer them – and, hopefully, the staff, too – a breath of fresh air. Setting boundaries is not my business. Discipline comes from the staff who are there for the children the whole time – they are carers, police, mothers… I want to be a catalyst for something else to happen that isn't to do with issues like drugs and violence or the bad experiences in their lives that drive them to such extremes. I want to show them that they can get pleasure and satisfaction out of a fairly superficial activity, which is about decoration, pattern, colour.

5 Dancing breaks

Centre	Lead staff	Project description	Beneficiaries	Artist(s)
Derby City Pupil Referral Unit Peartree House Derby PRU	Sue Bradley, Key Stage 4 Pupil Referral Team Leader, Special Education Needs Support Services (SENSS)	A 10-week breakdance programme to be held at Derby Dance Centre	15 pupils aged 11–14	Leonard Jackson and Paul Steadman, Dancers

My background is almost the same as some of these kids, to be honest. That's why it works. I'd always danced but when I left school I did more than ten years of dead-end jobs. I didn't go to dance school until I was 27. That's how long I left it. When I auditioned at the Northern School of Contemporary Dance, I had never seen a contemporary dance company, never done a ballet class, never had any formal training. I was just a street dancer – and break-dancing was my tradition.

A lot of people told me I should go but it took one woman – a social worker – to get tough with me. She told me to get my act together, though she didn't put it quite as politely as that. She got me the application form, got me to write it and got me to send it. That's why I kick ass here sometimes, because some of these young people have got major potential.

Leonard Jackson is 38 now, though he hardly looks it – the work, he jokes, is keeping him youthful. As Dance Development Worker at the Derby Dance Centre, his work is certainly full on, with a growing demand from young people, particularly young men and boys, for dance training. A male youth dance company created and based in Derby – Storm – has spawned several other such groups in the East Midlands. Over the years, word about the dynamic classes run by Leonard and his colleagues, both at the Centre and on site, has spread across the formal education sector and has now reached Derby's Special Education Needs Support Services, a.k.a. SENSS.

The deal between SENSS and the Dance Centre is for a ten-week pilot project, which is to be externally evaluated. Each week a mixed group of excluded young people at Key Stage 3, who attend a PRU group at Peartree House, come here for a morning class. The boys learn breakdance routines; the girls are keener on street dance.

While we wait for the group to arrive, Leonard and I talk about some of the challenges of the work. We are sitting in the café of the Dance Centre, which was converted from a bath house and an old Methodist church six years ago but which still looks glamorously fresh and airy. This setting seems a world away from the undistinguished, often shabby rooms of many of the exclusion units and schools I have been visiting. 'They would never come here normally,' Leonard says of the PRU group:

But this building is *for* them. If it hadn't been for those sorts of kids, we wouldn't be working here. The Centre would not be here. Yet, they'll walk past and say: that's not for me.

There is just time for a quick tour: dance studios discovered around corners and up stairs; corridors and walls set off by cool, commissioned sculptures; the sound of music from a room where a small-scale company is auditioning for a coveted 18-month residency here at the Centre; and doors opening into a well-appointed theatre where touring dancers regularly perform to the public. 'I like to show this to the kids,' Leonard smiles. 'I say "One day, you could be here… so, Be Good!"' Finally, the thumping of a boom box draws us to the ground floor studio where Leonard's protégé, David, is limbering up for the class. Leonard pushes the pause button and explains:

> This is their space. We couldn't do this class in school. If they were told to leave the room for some reason at school, they wouldn't care. Here, they would lose something special by having to leave, so they tend to stay focused.

Although there are around 15 young people in the dance group, only half turn up today. This is the hard core of the group, all burning to dance. Two of the boys are anxious to show off the moves they have been working on together since the last session. Another boy is here despite an injured arm, determined to carry on; 'frankly,' Leonard confides later, 'he isn't very good technically but his commitment is outstanding.' One of the girls, an inveterate complainer according to Leonard, turns up as usual to moan and dance with equal enthusiasm.

■ ■ ■

When I catch up with Leonard after the session, he describes the morning as 'fairly typical'.

> Little Paolo is fantastic – he never wants to stop. We taught them a little routine, then left them to develop it. You saw what he did with his partner. We put them together so that they would bounce off each other and it worked.

Thinking of how other groups have developed in the past, Leonard imagines aloud how tight-knit this group might become if it carries on into next term and beyond. 'They'll be able to do some really good stuff if

they all stick at it…' he says, then remembering the context, laughs ruefully and corrects himself. 'If they all stay back, basically.'

■ ■ ■

In some ways, teaching this kind of group is difficult. They are streetwise kids, that's how they know breakdancing, but, to be honest, they can be *too* streetwise sometimes. There are so many things going on with them and they can kick off for any reason. Last week, I had to pull the boys out of the class to watch a breakdance video to give them time to get it back together and come back to work. Same thing with a boy and a girl the week before. Yet, to be truthful, these are only minor tantrums and they're not usually caused by anything going on in here.

Leonard is wary of getting involved in any personal issues that the young people might bring in with them, preferring to keep his role to that of teacher and mentor. He knows, too, that he and David need to avoid being alone with a student: 'we don't know the history of these young people'. He leaves all that to those better trained to deal with it, though he is faintly troubled by the fact that he has never seen a male member of staff from SENSS accompanying the group. His own experience in dance has taught him that an adult male presence is usually helpful in working with boys and young men.

I ask him the question I have asked every artist so far: how does art – in this case, dance – help such students? What does it do? For Leonard, it is simple.

> Nothing you do is 'wrong', especially in something like breakdancing. Wherever you go with it, as long as you are true to its spirit, it is going to be 'right'. It is your personal signature. You are always going to be good at something. Even if you are not the best dancer, you may do a brilliant head-spin or back-spin. You are going to have some skill to be proud of.

On the other hand, Leonard does not see dance as a universal panacea. Dance is not necessarily the answer.

It's not just a question of throwing dance at the kids thinking that will work. If a kid's going to kick off, he'll kick off regardless of whether it's a breakdance class. Dance isn't going to work for everybody.

But, then, neither is mainstream education.

Larry loves breakdancing. He comes to the Wednesday evening class, all the way from Nottingham. He had been excluded from school but he went back in recently to try again. He was demonstrating his breakdancing skills in the school playground and a massive crowd gathered round to watch. He was thrown out for that. There may have been other things involved, but this is what he claims happened. My experience is that they kick kids out for the weakest reasons, for simple misdemeanours. It is tough to expect kids like Larry to go back to school and fit in straight away. It takes time. I know that these young people can be very difficult, but schools don't seem to have the time to reach them. It seems easier to get rid of them than to educate them. There's no thought about what happens to them after that.

Leonard's view that it is a 'messed up system' might sound unduly harsh, but it seems to be borne out by the huge pressures on SENSS itself, which is trying to cope with unpredictable but steadily growing numbers of exclusions. Most recent guidance on exclusions balances the needs of the individual pupil against the needs of the whole school community, but this can be influenced by media coverage. A high profile stabbing incident in Lincolnshire, to take a recent example, might mean automatic exclusion of anyone in the country found at school with a knife in their possession.

It is difficult to achieve 100 per cent timetables for so many pupils when they are unwilling or unable to cope in a traditional learning environment. This is why Sue Bradley, Key Stage 4 Pupil Referral Team Leader at SENSS and joint manager of the dance project, is keen to develop long-term relationships with artists and arts companies.

We struggle to recruit members of staff who can deliver this sort of work in this sort of curriculum, not just in performing arts but even in art and design. And yet that's what the kids want to do. When they are first excluded they come to me and I ask them: 'What did you like about school?' The answer is often: 'I loved drama' or 'Art at GCSE is the only subject I could do'. They are into PE and practical subjects. What they don't want is to sit at a desk in a classroom, as they've often failed in the more traditional learning environment.

When I push her for a more precise definition of what a project like that provided by Derby Dance Centre can offer these young people, Sue makes two important points. The first is that in the arts it is much easier to tailor what you are delivering to individual needs. There are no constraints in adapting the material to particular interests or abilities. The second point is that this kind of activity 'normalises' young people. They can invite their parents or carers to see them doing things they never had a chance to do at mainstream school, like taking part in an end-of-term show.

■ ■ ■

In rare cases, such projects can draw young people into a professional arts career. Leonard tells, probably not for the first time, David's inspirational story:

I met David when he was 14 at St Clare's, a special school for children with learning difficulties. He joined Storm and basically we couldn't get rid of him. We are now employing him as a trainee dance worker. As you saw this morning, he teaches breakdance and streetdance. He had fallen through the system and never learned how to read or write. Like me, he was dead-end-jobbing it, going nowhere, blagging his way through life. The only thing he stayed true to was dance. He got better and better and now he's easily one of the best teachers of dance around. Now that he's employed here, we have found him private tuition and he's having literacy classes. In the end, it has all come together for him.

Centre	Lead staff	Project description	Beneficiaries	Artist(s)
Bridgeway Centre Milber Junior School Newton Abbot Devon LSU	Liz Deane, Centre Manager	A project to enhance the appearance of the school by creating a mosaic mural	16 pupils aged 7–11	Devon Arts in Schools Initiative

6 Stop when you think it looks nice

Centre	Lead staff	Project description	Beneficiaries	Artist(s)
Rastrick High School Brighouse West Yorkshire LSU	Bev Peartree, Learning Centre Manager Kate Howell, Art teacher	A 3-week programme of workshops to produce vinyl banners to be displayed on internal and external walls of the school	36 pupils aged 12–15	Tom Wood, Painter

Rastrick High School in the Yorkshire town of Brighouse between Halifax and Huddersfield is older than it looks. A plaque on the wall of its reception area bears the date 1621. Formerly a voluntary-aided boys' grammar school, the kind I went to back in the 1960s, Rastrick became a 'voluntary controlled comprehensive school' in 1985. I wonder whether it has retained its seventeenth-century motto: *Puer non res est sed spes.* Roughly translated, this makes the claim that *A child is nothing but hope.*

■ ■ ■

The Learning Centre is not what I was expecting. Rather than a set of unremarkable rooms squirrelled away in the main school, the Centre is a brand new building; it opened in April 2002. Built of fresh cream brick, it is the antithesis of the traditional 'sin-bin' – a word I would hesitate to use except that staff here use it themselves, precisely to define what the Centre isn't. As I am toured around its generously proportioned suite of five rooms, including two arrayed with banks of computers (all 20-odd of them in active use), I learn to my astonishment that, when money was first made available to Calderdale for such a centre, not everyone saw it as a desirable addition. However, when I met the Headteacher later, she confirmed that, at Rastrick, an in-school learning centre was seen as a definite asset to the school.

Rather than thinking of it as an exclusion unit, the whole idea has been to promote the Centre as a place of learning where students are ultimately able to build relationships with the teachers and the subject areas they have had a 'barrier' with. Although there is a room here designated as an exclusion room, there has generally been no need to use it as such. Intervention strategies have been put in place so that students at risk can be identified and supported before they end up here.

Targeted at Key Stage 3 students, the Centre also links to alternative programmes at Key Stage 4. The purpose of the Centre is to reintroduce students to normal lessons and part of that is to provide 'enrichment activities'. The building has been designed to support creative and practical activities, including art, textile-making and cooking. Even English and Maths are delivered in a creative way, taking advantage of the smaller classes here. As a school, Rastrick has a strong tradition of arts work, which the Head has always seen as essential to the curriculum as well as to extra-curricular programmes.

One of the prime movers in the arts project that is nearing completion at the Centre is the art teacher, Kate Howell, who has come up here to work with the children and Tom Wood, the artist-in-residence. Kate has always been interested in Special Education Needs teaching, believing that art is a constructive way of working on all sorts of issues with children and build-ing up their confidence. Creative strategies developed from her early experience with 'disaffected' students have been transferable here.

> The arts are so successful because there's no right or wrong answer. A lot of these students' prob-lems come down to low confidence – whether the root cause is an actual learning difficulty or an inadequate home environment. Discovering that they can create something that you think is brilliant, and then seeing it pinned up on the classroom wall, can change their outlook instantly. Next time, they will remember what they achieved, so they try harder, and they move from hardly listening to you, because they're convinced they can't do it, to learning really quickly. Once the confidence is there, you can start to link it to other curriculum subjects like English; for example, an illustration for a poem will get them reading it without even realising.

Bev Peartree, the Centre Manager, agrees: 'A lot of these students are scared to try things because they are scared of failure. In a creative and open-ended project like this, that doesn't matter as you don't define work as right or wrong.'

Tom makes a similar point in talking about his own role as artist in this context: 'I don't feel I am coming in to say this is how you do it or that this is the only way. I see myself not so much passing on knowl-edge as saying: let's explore this together.'

■ ■ ■

Although he has come into the Centre as an artist rather than a teacher, Tom has done so much work in schools that he can act the teacher if he needs to control a class. He was for many years the Education Officer for Cartwright Hall, Bradford's city art gallery, where he also worked with young people in youth and out-of-school settings. This is his first time in an LSU, however.

> The hardest thing here is to keep them together as a group when they are all at such different levels; some are computer literate and on task, while others have very short attention spans.

The group he is working with at the moment is composed of a mixture of Centre students and 'gifted and talented' students from mainstream Art classes. The idea behind this is that, when the final work goes up around the school and people ask who has done it, it won't be instantly pigeonholed as by 'that lot' at the Learning Centre. 'We thought there might be divisions within this group,' Bev says, 'but they didn't segregate. They have produced high quality work – there's going to be a real 'wow' factor around the school that will challenge stereotypes and change perceptions about what people are capable of.'

According to Tom, the project is about owner-ship. At the moment it is contained within the Centre but it will shortly be out in the school, with peer groups looking at their work and judging it, so all the students are keen to do the best they can.

> It's a corny word but it will be empowering. It will give them a real sense of pride. For children who feel they are behind all the time, suddenly they will be ahead. They can say: 'I can do something that all those other kids can't.'

There have already been some dramatic improvements among the students. There has been full attendance right from the start, with Year 9s ready and waiting for the door to open each morning. According to Bev, once the project is complete, quite a few are set to go back into lessons they had been pulled out of.

> The Year 9s, who meet on Fridays, have moved on so much in how they work as a group and relate to each other. We would not have put them in the same room before but they are now coming up with ideas together, which is very good to see. Before, they were struggling with their options and how to fill up their timetables, but they now want to take the new GNVQ course in art and design.

However, the success of the project is judged here more on the difference it has made to the children personally than on their academic choices.

> Their confidence has grown unbelievably. Some from the first group are now the team leaders for

the third group, mentoring Years 7–9. They have the confidence to go off to the art department to use the computers there. Their whole *presence* has changed since they've been working on this. One student, who is being tested for dyslexia, was having considerable behaviour problems, but working with Tom for a few days has transformed him. He is concentrating hard and this has made a big difference not just here but back in his other classes, too.

Tom's own work is split between traditional painting using oils (he has had work exhibited at the National Gallery) and digital imagery. This project has allowed him to explore the potential links between the two. He reports, too, that he is also learning from the children.

> Today, for example, I have had two instances where someone has done something I didn't know was possible in Photoshop, although I've been using that programme since it came out. So, *my* knowledge has increased.

The rooms are full of vivid designs and print-outs pinned up on the walls and littering the tables. I sit alongside students who take me through the processes of Photoshop, manipulating drawings that they have scanned in. I learn from Bev what it is that is being created here.

> Although we had come up with the concept for the project, we felt it was important that the students worked it out for themselves. We took the children for a walk around the school, saying it looked a bit boring and how could we brighten it up? They soon came up with the idea that it would look better if we put up some posters or banners.

That idea has developed into the current plan to hang full-length vinyl banners outside nine locations in the school, including Humanities, PE, Science, Art, IT, Maths, English and the Learning Centre itself. The designs are based on objects and symbols associated with the various departments and disciplines. Tom explains how he has shifted the students from 'very low tech' methods like drawing and painting to 'very high tech' digital techniques – and back again.

> We started by doing simple silhouettes based on brainstorming sessions where they had to think of shapes and things they saw when they went into those parts of the school. For Art, for example, there was a list including paintbrush, palette, clay pots and so on. I asked them to use their sketchbooks first to explore how to convey each object through outline only. They cut each out and used them as simple stencils, which they did rubbings of. This was the raw material for the textures they were going to use, though I didn't tell them that until they had finished. They are quite interesting and attractive things in their own right, but they are just one step on a much longer journey.
>
> We then scanned in lots of objects as well as the sketches and created simple layering in basic Photoshop and printed the results out as a reference point. Today, we are doing more advanced work with Photoshop and at the same time moving back, almost to where we started. We are making interesting textures again by doing drawings based on computer printouts of their work. It's all about layers – it's a *process* that they are engaged in and not necessarily an end-product and, hopefully, a process that they can keep dipping in and out of. I'm trying to ensure that they understand that each bit of this process is really pushing them forward on this journey. There is a strong element of them just wanting to get there, so what you have to do is set them small individual tasks and keep reminding them that these will all lead to creating the banners.

The students' comprehension of this is, I discover, quite sophisticated. One comment in particular seems to convey a certain understanding of the experimental and provisional nature of the creative process:

> How do you know it's finished? You don't really – you just stop when you think it looks nice.

7 A bit gang-like

Centre	Lead staff	Project description	Beneficiaries	Artist(s)
Chesham Park Community College Chesham Buckinghamshire LSU	Catherine Lloyd, Inclusion Manager Jo Wright, Teaching Assistant	A project to devise and produce a video, originally conceived as a documentary to examine personal choices and challenges	6 pupils aged 14–15	The Mirror Circus Film Company

The football scene reminds me of *Reservoir Dogs*. It is beautifully shot. And I liked how they speak to camera at the end about their roles.

Yeah. I enjoyed the arrest, which we filmed at the youth club, especially the bit where I had to drag him outside. It's a bit gang-like. We need those bits of violence to give it a bit of a kick.

Yes... it is a very *male* film. Definitely not for Year 7s.

We are sitting in the Middle Room. It is, aptly enough, a kind of halfway house both academically and in the sense that it is a room through which others walk on their way to somewhere else in Chesham Park Community College. However, for the Year 9 and 10 boys gathered around the table – Simon, Matt, Derek, Tom, Alun and Ali – it is their main base.

This is, in fact, the Inclusion Unit, set up to reduce the incidence of exclusion at Key Stage 3. Catherine Lloyd is its manager. Jo Wright, one of two Teaching Assistants, is also at the table. While Catherine has a modest walk-on part, Jo takes the lead female role in *Welcome Home, Dad*, the film that the group has recently completed with the help of the Mirror Circus Film Company.

The film was premiered a few weeks ago but, as many of those invited were unable to make it thanks to a freak snowfall, the film is being shown again tonight. I have come early to meet the film-makers and find out a little more about the project. The discoveries I make as we talk are not just to do with the process of the project itself, but about the dynamic among the students, who manage, heroically, to survive at least an hour and a half of my questions before finally escaping.

One recurring theme in our rather meandering conversation is Des, who is late for this meeting and then later, and who ultimately fails to materialise. He is the main man from Mirror Circus and he is, according to the group, 'always late'. He rings eventually and apologises – he is stuck with technical problems on another project and can't make it, but he doesn't 'want the guys to think I don't care'. 'Too late for that, Mr Desmond,' says one of the group drolly when the message is relayed to us.

The group's gentle humour at Des' expense (I am also reliably informed that his hair 'sticks up like a tree') should not mask the excellent relationship he has built with the boys. 'I am not sure,' Catherine tells me afterwards, 'that many artists or companies would have stuck with the gang – us included – that long, let alone got so much out of them. Their behaviour was extremely challenging at times, even for someone like me used to being headteacher in a PRU! It was really Des' faith and persistence that got them through.'

The evidence of this is in the film itself; according to Catherine, no one had expected the final product to be as professional and impressive as it is.

■ ■ ■

The film's plot now turns around a father's decision to abandon a life of crime, but the first proposed storyline that the group had come up with concerned drug dealers. It had 'copious amounts of death and despair' in it, Catherine says. As time went on, however, the students themselves gradually refined the plot into a family drama around crime and redemption, and the scriptwriting and filming began. It all took over a year – with four weeks filming and four weeks in a London studio. There was a slight disappointment that the latter turned out to be 'more like someone's house' than the BBC and I think the group are keen to get more experience wielding the camera in future. However, the main focus for the students in this film was creating the script – and appearing in front of the camera.

There was real nervousness about being filmed – even now, one of the group is planning to 'go into hiding' to avoid the embarrassment of people seeing him in the film. According to Catherine, for the first few weeks they had a struggle to concentrate and work with each other, but then it started to come together.

> They have low literacy levels and so reading from a script was a real challenge. For them actually to be reading A4 sheets of words in front of each other in the last couple of weeks has been a huge step forward. At the beginning, they wouldn't have attempted this.

The growing confidence of the group can be seen in the film, which was filmed more or less in sequence. There is a marked change in pace from the first to the second half of the video.

> In the first half, lots of different things are happening, but then it becomes much clearer, with more well-defined characters and a sharper storyline. It mirrors how they developed as a group.

When Jo says this, it brings into focus the easy banter of the boys. They do relate well to each other. 'We got on but it wasn't easy,' says one about working together on the film. Now, as the staff remark, it is good to see them playing off each other, working as a group. They also point out something I had missed earlier: Matt had logged Simon off the computer which he had started up, so that he would pay better attention to our meeting.

> That was a *hugely* significant thing to do in front of the rest of the group.

If you are not working with these young people day in, day out, it would easy to miss that tiny glimpse of personal development.

The new-found maturity of the boys is reflected in the fact that Matt, Simon and Derek are to offer support to younger pupils. They are going to be involved in another short video aimed at Year 7s making the transition from primary school, to show them what secondary school is like. It will also link in with those Year 6s who it is known will need help and reassurance.

> Matt will handle the technical side, Derek will act – once upon a time, appearing in front of camera would have been totally out of character – and Simon is good with younger kids, so he will be a mentor.

■ ■ ■

Filming has kept these boys on an even keel and given them something to look forward to. They have agreed they are now going to stick it out here, one way or another, until the end of the school year.

8 Artists in a landscape

Centre	Lead staff	Project description	Beneficiaries	Artist(s)
The Margaret Glen-Bott School Wollaton Park Nottingham LSU	Helen Allan, LSU Manager Rachael Phelps, Community Arts Coordinator	A visual arts project to encourage expression and communication through 2D and 3D art forms	10 pupils aged 11–12	Jed Brignal, David Roach, Liz Sparks and Kelly Monk, Visual artists Donovan Pennant, Filming and photography

There's quite a professional atmosphere in there. When you go in, you'll feel like you've walked into an artist's studio.

Rachael Phelps is right. The room is filled with activity. About ten pupils are distributed around the large art room working with not one, but five visual artists.

The first group I meet is working on a large painting of the Nottingham cityscape. They tell me that it is based on a photograph taken from a high point near the Victoria Centre. There is a fine building there, from which you can look over the entire city. The photograph was traced and the image magnified with a projector onto this large sheet, where the image was again traced out. The current task is now to complete the colouring and detail of this impressive panorama. There is a sense of mild urgency as the whole project is meant to be completed at next week's session. All the work here is then to be put on public display; Rachael is in conversation with three galleries, including the Lakeside Arts Centre at Nottingham University, and there are plans afoot for a tour of the show to local primary schools.

■ ■ ■

As Community Arts Coordinator, Rachael's post at the Margaret Glen-Bott School is unique in the city. Her responsibilities, as her title suggests, extend beyond this school, to the wider community, including institutions of higher education. She has a small teaching commitment but spends most of her time developing arts projects in schools. Evidence of her programme at Margaret Glen-Bott – for which she has a budget of £30,000 to be spent over two years – can be found at the entrance to the school, where a stained-glass window has been installed. Designed by pupils, the window was first displayed for a month at Waterstone's bookshop.

Prior to taking up this post three years ago, Rachael was working in Liverpool and she contrasts the 'forward-thinking' strategies there with the way in which arts education programmes are regarded in schools like this one, which are operating at the margins of the official criteria for success set nationally. Margaret Glen-Bott has had a rough ride over the last few years. There have been two Ofsteds, the first identifying serious weaknesses, the second putting the school on special measures. Now the DfES has announced that the school will close next summer. The main reason is that the school is financially unviable due to falling rolls and thus unable to provide a wide curriculum. Yet admissions are still high, significantly swollen by a large population of children of asylum seekers and of 'transient' families (the school is located between Nottingham's two universities). These children – nearly 100 of them this year, not including the Year 7 intake – are often unable to go to other schools because they are all full; this school, therefore, has more than its fair share of pupils with social and emotional difficulties. Some find themselves, at least temporarily, in Interlink, the LSU here, and they are the focus of Rachael's current project.

Helen Allan, Interlink Manager, believes that learning support is all about tackling 'the behaviour that gets in the way of learning'. She reels off a list of the problems, 'bereavement, family breakdown, medical problems…', which create 'a constant low level of disruption and attention seeking, temper tantrums and so on'. She cites a boy who was already experiencing severe cultural adjustment and language problems when his father decided to leave the family home.

The aim of Interlink is reintegration of its students into mainstream classes. Helen mentions a 14-year-old girl from Year 9 who was a school non-attender. She began part-time attendance at the LSU and now turns up to school full time; she will take some lessons with the Unit, go with a teaching assistant to others, and to the rest on her own. The approach to achieving such successes, however, is 'needs driven', that is, therapeutic rather than curriculum-based. If a child arrives in an upset state, he or she will not be expected to embark immediately on a Maths lesson, for example, though a little such teaching might be introduced later on in the day.

There are four learning and behaviour support staff working in and out of class. They have trained to Level 1 Counselling and taken related courses; two hope to go on 'dyslexia training' soon. Therapies include de-escalation techniques to help with anger management and 'giving the kids space'. Somewhat controversially, the Unit has also tried 'modelling' – working on the attitudes of other staff; as Helen remarks, if a teacher says that a student is mad and shouldn't be there, it's not only the child that has a problem.

> We have a tremendous amount of freedom to do what we think we must do when it is appropriate to do it. The attitudes of other staff are moving on from the 'I don't want him in my class anymore – oh good, Interlink has picked him

up' position. They can see our methods working, for example, in the case of Colin, whose behaviour was horrendous; he was on the verge of being permanently excluded. We took him through his SATs and found him a college placement for 18 months – he's actually a bright lad. He is now going to sit three papers at GCSE. I mentioned this at a review meeting recently and his old teachers did a double take. Him? Doing an exam? He's going to be in the hall with all those other students? In fact, I expect him to get Cs. He's achieved something that they never expected.

■ ■ ■

So, it must have been an easy decision for Helen to agree to Rachael's proposal for an arts project on the theme of 'identity and environment'. A Year 7 group, affected by issues of transition from primary to secondary school, was chosen from Interlink's 'at risk' register. Rachael takes up the story.

> We were seeking a project that would enable these children to achieve something and allow us to celebrate that success in quite a public, high-profile way. Our hope was that their behaviour would change, not necessarily in a quantifiable way but *qualitatively*. We wanted them to have an experience of success which they would always remember.

No doubt the planned exhibition will be a source of great pride, with the children's parents and carers and friends turning up to admire the work that they have made. When I suggest that the creative process of getting to that point of celebration will make a lasting impact on them and their confidence in their own abilities, Helen is, properly, more cautious in her assessment of the potential of such a project to affect deep-rooted behaviours:

> It's too early to say there have been changes as a result of the project, as there are so many factors affecting these children. They went on a trip to see artists at work at Patchings Art Centre out at Calverton and they came back with their eyes on stalks, but they might equally have been having

a good time because they'd had a better week-end at home. It's difficult to quantify the effect and say that we made that difference, but they do seem to be enjoying it and getting a lot out of it. No one has dropped out.

Given the apparent success of the project, it seems ironic that the school is closing, especially as the education authority is taking an interest in the project at a fairly senior level; an officer researching exclusion is expected to visit. It is sad, too, that the new school due to take over the site has its own criteria for entry and a new catchment area, so students here will have to be shipped off to another site, seven miles away.

■ ■ ■

The youngest professional artist here today is David Roach, who has just completed an MA art course at DeMontfort University in Leicester. David has no teaching experience and had no opportunity to do an education placement during his course, but he is keen to work with young people. He is on a steep learning curve here. The two girls working with him are bright, I have been told, but they have been so badly bullied that they have lost their confidence and withdrawn into themselves. They are working on a photographic construction.

Having taken some pictures of the school grounds, they are now making a three-dimensional environment. When I come over to chat, they are at the point of inserting figures into this rural landscape. 'They look familiar,' I say. They smile, as do their photographic selves, taking up their places and becoming visible through the trees.

9 A shop of feelings

Centre	Lead staff	Project description	Beneficiaries	Artist(s)
Pupil Development Centre Woodlands Primary School Leeds LSU	Karen Shotton, Centre Manager	A series of drama workshops, to be observed by 4 other regional centres for dissemination	60 pupils aged 8–9	Yorkshire Women's Theatre

The urban fabric buckles and decays as we pass from the city centre into a wasteland of bleak housing blocks, many with windows boarded up. I am told later that this is a notorious area for street crime. The most popular form of mugging, it seems, is to smash someone's car window as they wait at traffic lights and then drag them out of the car. Hard drugs are also rife and have become a serious problem in primary schools here, among children as young as eight.

■ ■ ■

Leeds has been divided into five 'wedges'; in each wedge is a Primary Pupil Development Centre. Karen Shotton is Centre Manager of the Pupil Development Centre in the East Wedge, which is a well appointed and spacious new building located – like the other four centres – in a working school. Here the school is Woodlands Primary, also recently built on the site. Although the Centre is a separate unit, parked outside the main building, its links with the school and its staff and pupils are very close.

> We are very much part of school life here; every child will come down into the Centre at some point. It is not a place 'where the naughty ones are sent', but where each pupil will come at some point to address social and emotional issues. Where our model for PLSUs (Primary Learning Support Units) differs from practice in other parts of the country is that we offer an outreach service as well, covering the whole of Leeds, from leafy lane to inner city.

Each centre has a team of outreach workers, whose brief is to service all the other schools in its particular wedge. The philosophy behind this system, Karen explains, is that it is 'not realistic' to take children out of their own schools and transfer them to a centre somewhere else. It would be creating a false environment for them when what they need is to survive happily among their own peers. There are always reintegration issues if children are removed.

The three outreach workers based at Woodlands will each be called out to schools in the area. A room will have been designated for them to deliver a programme of work to children chosen by the school, always with a member of school staff participating. As they cannot get to all the children who need their intervention yet, the priority is to support lower Key Stage 2 children (aged 7–9) as an early intervention strategy. Karen explains that working collaboratively with a member of staff at the outreach school 'facilitates the continuation of the work and spread of good practice'.

Each visit is different. If there has been a bereavement, they will try to deal with loss through a variety of visualisations and discussing analogous events, such as losing a pet. More often, the problem is anger: Karen admits that a lot of the children she deals with are angry 'for one reason or another'. Sessions always aim to end with some celebration and empowerment of the young people.

Coordination between centre managers and staff at the five PDCs is close and regular. They meet every two weeks to pool information and share good practice. Thus, the current drama project at Woodlands, run by Yorkshire Women's Theatre, is being watched carefully by other centres with the open intention of adapting the company's techniques and approaches in their own future work.

> This drama project is another string to our bow. Another tool in the toolbox. If children are not accessing the curriculum, why give them more of it? We must find a way of tuning them back in. Drama works very well in this area. For one thing, it is all about making the right choices. And when they enjoy the experience, it can motivate them to explore further the issues that are being acted out.

Working in a neighbourhood that is one of the worst in the country for literacy and numeracy levels, Karen is not complacent about the importance of teaching basic skills, but she believes that a child's social and emotional receptivity can be a crucial factor in the success or failure of that teaching. She takes a proactive approach to changing behaviour – and drama, she believes, is an effective route towards that. If children can be turned on to learning through projects like these, it will, she says, open the door to all the better things in life.

> Drama offers a safe environment where children can reinvent what has personally happened to them. They can put in a different, more positive ending. There is the chance to enter the realm of fantasy where they get to be the person they'd like to be. They might have been bullied for months, but here they can try out being the confident person who can deal effectively with bullies – or even play the bully themselves.

A lot of the pupils that Karen and her colleagues work with are emotionally withdrawn, 'invisible' children, easily lost in the mainstream system.

> Teachers will say that they could do with a class full of pupils like these, but in fact they are not reaching their full potential. They are not socialising. And they are not accessing the curriculum.

Karen is pleased that some of these pupils have now been able to make some progress through participating in the drama project. I later witness the theatre company in action, involving nine-year-old pupils in devising a drama about the dangers of drugs. Karen tells me about one of the children who asked a question during a hot-seating (where another pupil takes the role of a protagonist in the play). Rachel, in fact, has profound speech problems yet here she was, adding her voice to a public conversation. Her speech therapist is convinced that drama offers a possible solution for Rachel's difficulties. Previously withdrawn and quiet, she now feels it is safe to speak.

■ ■ ■

> I don't think we do anything radical here. Ours is a commonsense approach to reconnecting these children. We base our work on building intrinsic motivation. If we can trigger that in a child, they can take it into any situation they find themselves in.

As Karen explains it, such motivation cannot be engineered through any kind of formal reward system. The reward has to come from within the child and should last a lifetime. She knows this goes against the conventional wisdom of some professionals, who have created complex systems of carrot and stick, but often the most important people in a child's world, those at home, fail to recognise or validate such rewards, thus nullifying any benefit they might have conferred.

Her approach here and on other issues seems rather different from that of a conventional teacher's and, indeed, Karen turns out not to be a trained teacher but a former nursery nurse. She was appointed, she believes, because her focus was not too curriculum-led – her ethos is more holistic:

When I see a child, I see a whole child and I wonder how to take that whole child forward. A teacher, on the other hand, may look at the same child and wonder what the best way might be to get that child writing.

Her emphasis on emotional care is perhaps best exemplified by her occasional theatrical performances as the proprietor of a 'shop of feelings'. All I get to see of this dramatic side to Karen is a box full of coloured cloth and materials, loaded into the trunk of her car, ready for her next 'show', but she tells me that she appears in class as a thickly accented foreign lady, dressed in 'a flouncy skirt and a silly hat'.

■ ■ ■

Having captured her young audience's attention, she begins bartering her motley collection of velvet and cotton swatches. She starts by introducing the language of feelings – 'courage', for example. She selects a piece of red velvet. This is a cloak of courage. Wrap it around you and feel the courage inside. What have you got lots of inside that you can give me in exchange? The boy looks uncertain, so the other children are asked. A girl pipes up: he is always kind to me. Well then, you can give me a bit of kindness for this cloak of courage.

It is multi-sensory. You let them sit down with the cloak around them and hope that in future they will recall that feeling of courage instilled in them by wearing it.

What are you going to use your cloak of courage for? When I'm pushed over in the playground.

We are not into 'opening things up'; that's where specialists come in. But it is extraordinary what children will come out with. Once, a little boy got up and asked for love… and he chose to give me sadness back.

Centre	Lead staff	Project description	Beneficiaries	Artist(s)
Dalton Foljambe Learning Centre Dalton Rotherham LSU	Jean Poyser, Lead Teacher	An expressive dance project linked to PHSE work on feelings and emotions	10 pupils aged 9–10	Aujke Delnooz and Louise Parker, Dancers Charlie Illingworth, Visual artist

10 Choosing wild flowers

Centre	Lead staff	Project description	Beneficiaries	Artist(s)
London Borough of Richmond Pupil Referral Service Strathmore Centre Teddington Middlesex PRU	Hilary Dodman, Head of Pupil Referral Service Norman Crisp, Project worker	Working with a visual artist to design and make a wall mural for the outside recreation area, which is being turned into a garden	up to 24 pupils aged 14–16	Jenny Irish, Visual artist

It is a long way from Richmond station to the Strathmore Centre in Teddington. My visits to this area of London have always centred on gardens of one kind or another. Kew is not far away, nor are the formal gardens of Hampton Court. Such rural scenes flash past and we are somewhere altogether bleaker and more suburban.

Hilary Dodman, who is in charge of the Strathmore Centre, is unavoidably late for our appointment so I cool my heels at a large, round table in a large, bare room containing kitchen units. It feels as if the place is deserted. It turns out, when Hilary arrives, that we have indeed been abandoned. She had asked two of her students to stay on after lunch to meet and talk with me but both have absconded. I now vaguely recall seeing a figure in the entrance hall, lingering there before, it turns out, taking off for the afternoon.

■ ■ ■

The intake at Strathmore is around a dozen 14–16 year olds who are not attending mainstream school. Even when they have been permanently excluded, however, the first thing that the Centre does is to try to negotiate them back into the system. In a few cases, this is appropriate – where, for example, a student has been involved in a one-off incident – but, for most, Strathmore is, in effect, their last hope for getting back

on track with their young lives. One short-term future seems to be symbolised by the building on the adjoining site, beyond the fence, which houses the YOT. Strathmore works directly with some of the young people there, who have been through the courts and are under sentence or reparation order. Hilary is fully aware of just how much at risk her own students are.

> By the time these young people get to Strathmore, they are very damaged people. You could think of this place as a hospital which they have been referred to. What we are involved in is a restorative programme.

One of two centres within the Richmond upon Thames Pupil Referral Service, Strathmore was, in fact, an 'intermediate treatment centre' run by Social Services for troubled young people for around 20 years. Even now, the Centre has 'project workers' as well as teachers: people trained in youth and social work rather than education. Hilary is trying to shift the ethos from what was a drop-in centre to somewhere more purposeful in terms of education. However, in managing this transition, she is finding it very useful to have immediate access to Social Services staff, which most other PRUs do not have. It is, like the other centre, which deals with younger (Key Stage 3) students, a 'fragile environment'.

■ ■ ■

Later in the day, having been out with two other staff to view the plot that young people here are planning to transform into a garden over the next few months, we all sit and talk about some of the characters at the Centre. One, in particular, seems to embody the strange juxtapositions of anger and equally sudden deference found among many of the students here – one moment kicking off, snapping a pool cue in two or ripping up a drawing, the next politely apologising for bumping into a member of staff. It sounds like a confusing, tough environment for an artist. It reminds me of a phone conversation with another centre where the teacher had taken stress-related leave largely because of the 'appalling' way in which her class had treated the artists and their well-meaning attempts to engage with the students.

Hilary describes the different ways in which the two artists involved in this Centre's project have reacted to the challenging behaviour of their students. A few sessions in, the guest landscape gardener had apparently decided enough was enough. He has not returned. For staff, this is 'perfectly understandable', blame hardly appropriate. As Hilary says, for someone to come in once a week is much harder than being there every day, learning who the students are, how they behave and how they react, what works and what doesn't – seeing them, finally, as individuals with individual needs. It is a simple fact that not everyone can handle a situation like this. On the other hand, Jenny Irish, the artist responsible for creating a mural with the group, *has* found a way of inserting herself into their lives.

Jenny is young and finds talking to our students fairly easy. She also understands that she has to be very active herself, doing a lot of stuff before these young people will engage. They will probably refuse at first, because they don't understand what's going on. They don't know what you're asking them to do and they don't have the confidence to move things forward themselves. If *you* are busy, they will eventually get stuck in, but, if you just stand there and wait for the difficult behaviour to stop before you

get started, nothing will happen. Jenny has the right idea. She began painting the wall so that there was something to show the young people when they arrived – next week, she said, *you* can get involved.

■ ■ ■

Having lost the gardener, a project worker – Norman Crisp – has now stepped enthusiastically into the breach. He takes us outside to view the recreation area designated for the proposed garden. It is the size of a suburban backyard and lies behind a garage-cum-workshop building, the wall of which will be painted over with a mural. The ground has been cleared; all that remains is a beech tree at the other end, against the fence.

We have an outline plan which the young people have designed. They've been doing a lot of research, cutting pictures out of magazines, drawing and sketching, brainstorming. We visited Kew Gardens, Bushy Park, Hampton Court and they took photographs. Quite a few of them have come up with similar ideas about what should be included: somewhere to sit, a water feature of some sort, even lights. Along the back edge we are going to have a raised area. Some of the lads are designing a seat to go around the tree, which they'll make in our carpentry workshop. We will put some sort of surface down so it can be walked over – grass is out, because it would need regular mowing, so they've suggested those blue chippings or pebbles or stones. Of course, we have to be careful here about health and safety – and that the material cannot be used as a weapon or to break windows.

Pointing to the lower area in front of us, Norman explains that the young people are keen that it is kept as natural as possible. They have suggested daffodils, snowdrops, bluebells and foxgloves for the spring and early summer. They are now looking at what plants might bloom later in the year. The water feature will be part of a paved area, where it will benefit from the power supply from the garage (installed for welding workshops). There will be terracotta pots, which the students will be glazing and then covering in mosaics, and hexagonal wooden tubs, which again will be made in carpentry sessions. A student suggested that log rolls could be used for a low fence to define the front edge of the garden, which abuts the tarmac of the playground.

Staff agree that the students have put a lot of thought into the project, coming up with some inspired ideas and are keen to start matching their vision with the realities of the practical design and building work. Jenny has taken pictures of the wall with a digital camera so that they can explore different mural concepts on screen before applying the paint; she wants each of them to have a bit of the wall that they can call their own. Back in the main building, Norman displays the first results of a foraging trip to the local scrap yard. A rusty fan from a car is being welded into a sculpture for eventual display in the garden.

The project may well contribute to the young people's future in terms of qualifications; the Centre, which 'disapplied' (opted out) from the National Curriculum (though GCSE English, Maths, Art and PSHE are still available), is particularly enthusiastic about the potential of the less academic and more evidence-based approach of ASDAN (Awards Scheme Development and Accreditation Network). More profound, however, is the potential impact on these young people of seeing a garden emerge from wasteland, as a result of their imaginative ideas and physical labour.

■ ■ ■

No one is less tolerant or more critical of their 'failures'

than the young people themselves. Norman shows me a small display of photographs from a previous project with Orleans House Gallery. There would be more pictures, he says, but some students cannot stand the sight of their own portrait. If a photograph went up, they would get very upset and take it down. Hilary gives an example of how such students torment themselves with an impossible standard of perfection.

> Everything he does has to be absolutely perfect. He spends an age doing a picture and then, before I can stop him, he rips it to pieces. It's something to do with approval. They have had to live with a lot of failure on paper. They want the gratification of it being right but they are afraid that it won't match up to their expectations, no matter what you say.

Their commitment to the idea of the garden gives some hope. Norman puts it well: 'If they can transform this patch of ground, then maybe they can transform aspects of themselves.'

As Norman recalls the suggestion made by one young person that a signpost could be planted to guide people to the various sections of the garden, as if this were indeed Kew or Hampton Court, I look over at the neighbouring building, beyond the garden, where the Youth Offending Team is based, and remember an earlier remark of his – one that lingers.

> They specifically said that they didn't want just cultivated flowers planted here. They wanted *wild* flowers in their garden, too.

1 Projects visited

Centre	Lead staff	Project description	Beneficiaries	Artist(s)
Page 10 Integrated Support Service Centre Langdon Hills Basildon Essex PRU	Sharon Wilson, Assistant Manager Tim Moynihan, Senior Teacher Neil Finbow, ICT Maggie Torrie, Drama Sue Reeves, English Anne Ash, Art Sue Charlton, Primary and Music	Cultural Fusion, a series of multi-disciplinary arts workshops run over half a term on the theme of Africa and the Caribbean	80–100 pupils aged 5–16	Charlie Wilson, Storyteller Sol Ogundipe, The Afro Centre Mick Hutton, Musician (steel pan) Scott Irving, Graffiti artist Thabani Nyoni, Wise Moves Dance Malo Sonka, Drummer Heritage Ceramics
Page 30 Rastrick High School Brighouse West Yorkshire LSU	Bev Peartree, Learning Centre Manager Kate Howell, Art teacher	A 3-week programme of workshops to produce vinyl banners to be displayed on internal and external walls of the school	36 pupils aged 12–15	Tom Wood, Painter
Page 33 Chesham Park Community College Chesham Buckinghamshire LSU	Catherine Lloyd, Inclusion Manager Jo Wright, Teaching Assistant	A project to devise and produce a video, originally conceived as a documentary to examine personal choices and challenges	6 pupils aged 14–15	The Mirror Circus Film Company
Page 25 Derby City Pupil Referral Unit Peartree House Derby PRU	Sue Bradley, Key Stage 4 Pupil Referral Team Leader, Special Education Needs Support Services (SENSS)	A 10-week breakdance programme to be held at Derby Dance Centre	15 pupils aged 11–14	Leonard Jackson and Paul Steadman, Dancers

Centre	Lead staff	Project description	Beneficiaries	Artist(s)
Page 17 Didcot Girls' School Didcot Oxfordshire LSU	Sarah Pignéguy, Support Centre Coordinator	A project to make a film about living in Didcot	9 pupils aged 13–15	Elise Ahmed, RAP Community Action Ltd
Page 22 The Pewley Centre Guildford Pupil Referral Unit Surrey PRU	Pippa Morris, Head of Centre	Creating a large tile mural for the entrance of the PRU through 12 one-day workshop sessions	16 pupils aged 11–14	Liliana Montoya, Ceramicist
Page 38 Pupil Development Centre Woodlands Primary School Leeds LSU	Karen Shotton, Centre Manager	A series of drama workshops, to be observed by 4 other regional centres for dissemination	60 pupils aged 8–9	Yorkshire Women's Theatre
Page 14 Primary Assessment Centre for Education (PACE) St Helens Merseyside PRU	Margaret Simpson, Teacher in charge	A project based around a number of textile techniques, including felt making and collage, with inset sessions	16 pupils aged 7–11	Amy Robinson, Textile artist
Page 42 London Borough of Richmond Pupil Referral Service Strathmore Centre Teddington Middlesex PRU	Hilary Dodman, Head of Pupil Referral Service Norman Crisp, Project worker	Working with a visual artist to design and make a wall mural for the outside recreation area, which is being turned into a garden	up to 24 pupils aged 14–16	Jenny Irish, Visual artist
Page 35 The Margaret Glen-Bott School Wollaton Park Nottingham LSU	Helen Allan, LSU Manager Rachael Phelps, Community Arts Coordinator	A visual arts project to encourage expression and communication through 2D and 3D art forms	10 pupils aged 11–12	Jed Brignal, David Roach, Liz Sparks and Kelly Monk, Visual artists Donovan Pennant, Filming and photography

2 Projects photographed

Centre	Lead staff	Project description	Beneficiaries	Artist(s)
Page 8 The Burlington Centre Newtown Birmingham PRU	Mandy Finney, Learning Support	A project aiming to produce posters containing poetry and photographic images on the theme of 'my community'	8 pupils aged 11–14	Levi Tafari, Poet David Petts, Photographer Karen McDonnell, Designer
Pages 20–21 Pupil Referral Service North Secondary Brookside Mobile Unit Lancaster PRU	Frances Holland, Teacher	A 6-week project, Soundcard, based on songwriting, percussion and the production of a recording	10 pupils aged 11–14	More Music, Morecambe
Pages 28–29 Bridgeway Centre Milber Junior School Newton Abbot Devon LSU	Liz Deane, Centre Manager	A project to enhance the appearance of the school by creating a mosaic mural	16 pupils aged 7–11	Devon Arts in Schools Initiative
Page 41 Dalton Foljambe Learning Centre Dalton Rotherham LSU	Jean Poyser, Lead Teacher	An expressive dance project linked to PHSE work on feelings and emotions	10 pupils aged 9–10	Aujke Delnooz and Louise Parker, Dancers Charlie Illingworth, Visual artist

Richard Ings is a freelance writer and researcher in the arts with a particular interest in young people and creativity. Among his publications are *The Arts Included*, a report on the conference that launched the First Time Projects programme (Nick Randall Associates: 2002); *Mapping Hidden Talent*, the first book to examine grassroots youth music projects across the UK (The Prince's Trust/National Youth Agency: 1998); *Creativity: Caught or Taught?* on new creative approaches to the school curriculum (CAPE UK: 2000); *Funky on your Flyer* on extending young people's access to cultural venues (Arts Council England: 2001); *Taking it seriously: Youth arts in the real world* (National Youth Agency: 2002); and *Connecting Flights: Debating Globalisation, Diaspora and the Arts* (British Council: 2003). Most recently, NESTA has published *The Inventive Answer*, an essay on creativity and young people (2004).

Adrian Fisk began his photographic career documenting the road protest movement in England in the mid 1990s. He went on to record the illegal rave scene in London then moved further afield to work in India where among various subjects he has documented the human hair trade, dowry abuse and the night rat killers of Bombay. He is a member of the international collective of street photographers In-Public.com. His work has appeared in many magazines including the *Guardian Weekend*, the *Independent*'s Saturday and Sunday magazines, *ID* and *Eight* and a variety of publications across Europe.